# Creating a Roadmap out of Poverty for Americans with Disabilities: The Relationship of the Employment and Training Administration's Workforce Development System and Local Asset-Building Coalitions

# TABLE OF CONTENTS

# Executive Summary

For many years individuals with disabilities have been less likely to be employed than their working age nondisabled peers. The demographic profile for disability cuts across race, gender, age, and geography. Individuals with disabilities are more likely to be unbanked (30%) and to underutilize tax provisions because of a lack of knowledge about the Earned Income Tax Credit, or due to fear of losing important benefits such as health care. They are almost three times as likely to live in poverty as any other group.

The Workforce Investment Act, which became effective on July 1, 2000, has opened doors to unprecedented opportunities for jobseekers with disabilities to receive assistance and intensive services to match abilities and interests with employer needs. The U.S. Department of Labor's Office of Disability Employment Policy (ODEP), also advances opportunities for jobseekers with disabilities by providing national leadership in policy development that works to enhance employment profitability and advance economic self-sufficiency. ODEP accomplishes this through partnering with strategic stakeholders in asset development, developing research and training materials and financial education, and testing best practices through national policy demonstration projects. This white paper is an example of ODEP's research into best practices in asset development.

New strategies are being pioneered across the country that address both the challenges of advancing employment options for individuals with disabilities and moving forward with options to advance their economic security and self-sufficiency. Collaboration between One-Stop Career Centers, the Disability Program Navigators (DPNs,) and Asset Building Coalitions are reaching out to low-income workers with disabilities to help them to utilize the Earned Income Tax Credit (EITC), financial education, and other savings and asset building options. DPNs are staff in over 40 states who help job seekers with disabilities navigate the local and state public systems of services to find the help they need to become employed and reach economic self-sufficiency. ETA and the Social Security Administration (SSA) jointly fund, implement, and evaluate this initiative designed to improve the workforce investment system's capacity to service customers with disabilities and employers.

During the past three years, through a national campaign being led by the Internal Revenue Service (IRS) and the National Disability Institute (NDI), individuals with disabilities have been encouraged to think about a better economic future that begins with participation in the workforce. The campaign, called "The Real Economic Impact Tour," is raising expectations about the value of work, saving, and asset building.

This report focuses on three cities: Detroit, Jacksonville and Milwaukee, and the tie-in between the workforce development system and advancing self-sufficiency for individuals with disabilities. These three diverse cities, in partnership with their local free tax preparation and asset building coalition and the Workforce Development Centers, DPNs, and/or One Stop Career Centers, have partnered to educate and assist people with disabilities to:

- Break down barriers to employment;
- Understand the benefits available to them in the tax code through tax credits and tax deductions;
- Obtain free tax preparation and electronic filing and
- Begin the journey to self-sufficiency.

The Disability Initiatives in Detroit, Jacksonville and Milwaukee were supported by resources from the Real Economic Impact Tour and leveraged additional support through the volunteer efforts and involvement of their local One-Stop Career Centers and/or Workforce Development Centers. This collaboration paves the way out of poverty toward independence and self-determination for many working taxpayers with disabilities.

The Law Health Policy and Disability Center, at the University of Iowa, College of Law, conducted phone interviews with six cities and chose three that are using either their One Stop Career Centers or Workforce Development Centers to provide volunteer free tax preparation to citizens in their communities during the tax preparation season each year. A number of Centers are distributing information about asset building programs in their communities, but the three cities chosen for this Report are actually using their sites and often their staff during non-work hours to provide free tax preparation. Phone interviews were also conducted with members of the free tax coalition to understand how this unique model began. Findings from this qualitative review include:

- The Workforce Development Center can serve as a hub for volunteer tax preparation assistance and for financial education programs.
- Staff at the One-Stops can be trained to serve as volunteer tax preparers and to help connect job seekers with disabilities with other asset building options.
- DPNs are vital conduits for making One-Stop staff aware of financial education and asset development opportunities for people with disabilities, and for creating the linkages that expand local asset development partnerships.
- The Workforce Development system is an important collaborator with other community-based groups and entities (for-profit and not-for-profit) that can connect employment objectives with longer-term economic self-sufficiency goals.

*Recommendations for future action include consideration of:*

- Development of training and technical assistance to all One-Stops and Workforce Development Centers and state and local Workforce Investment Boards about the link between employment and asset building tools and strategies, with an expanded role for Centers as a hub for information, tax preparation assistance and financial education;
- Creation of pilot sites to bring together disability specific agencies and generic groups committed to implementing a comprehensive plan to advance economic self-sufficiency for working adults with disabilities, which documents individual and system change and impact;
- Identification of opportunities for policy development that stimulate a return to work, asset building options, and changes to the asset limits that allow continued coverage for healthcare and other essential public assistance;
- Organization of a state-level work group to bring public and private stakeholders together to identify opportunities for collaboration with the workforce development system that would expand activities to include but not be limited to: financial benefit planning, financial education, providing access to a number of refundable tax credits such as the Earned Income Tax Credit, and use of matched savings programs (for example, Individual Development Accounts (IDA)).

## Introduction to the Problem

In 2008, a majority of Individuals with significant disabilities remain outside of the workforce and often face multiple barriers to employment. One-Stop Career Centers, administered under the Workforce Investment Act, offer new opportunities to support jobseekers with disabilities to advance their employment and economic status. Demonstration and research activities funded by the Office of Disability Employment Policy (ODEP) and the Employment and Training Administration (ETA) at the US Department of Labor have pioneered new strategies to increase access to and effective participation of individuals with disabilities in the Workforce Development system.

However, achievement of an employment outcome and low-income wages fails to focus needed attention on possible strategies to advance the worker from poverty to a path to economic self-sufficiency. The mission of the U.S. Department of Labor (USDOL) is to promote the welfare of the job seekers, wage earners, and retirees of the United States by improving their working conditions, and advancing their opportunities for profitable employment. The vision of USDOL is to promote the economic well being of workers and their families and help them share the American Dream. For the first time, new community partnerships that involve the workforce development system are raising expectations for working age adults with disabilities about the importance of work, saving and asset building. This report offers promising evidence that a new set of partnerships at a national, state, and local level are targeting individuals with disabilities to advance employment and economic status.

The IRS Wage & Investment Benchmark study found that there are 5.0 million taxpayers with disabilities ages 18 to 59 who filed tax returns and when it compared their findings to the American Community Survey for the same age distribution found there were 6.6 million employed persons with a disability representing 6.3 million households.[1] When IRS Wage and Investment Research analyzed the American Community Survey in tandem with its Benchmark Study they demonstrated that a possible 1.3 to 1.6 million more tax returns could be filed from working residents ages 18 to 59.[2] This finding did not imply that the non-filers had any requirement to file a return. However, we now know that over a million taxpayers with disabilities that are not filing could be missing out on a number of refundable tax credits they are owed, even if working only a few hours a week or as a single filer.[3] In addition, the Benchmark study found that taxpayers with disabilities were more likely to be between the ages of 46 and 59; less likely to be college educated than their non-disability colleague (28% versus 52%); more likely to be retired than non-disability taxpayers (28% versus 9%); less likely to use a computer at home than non-disabled respondents (59% versus 76%); and less likely to invest than non-disabled taxpayers (70% versus 88%).[4]

In addition the Benchmark study reported that the Adjusted Gross Income of a taxpayer with a disability was $19,100 compared to $33,800 for a worker without a disability and that wages for a taxpayer with a disability were $15,000 compared to $39,300 for a worker without a disability. [5]

Working individuals and family members with disabilities recognize that work fulfills the need to be productive, enhances self-esteem, and expands opportunities for community participation. However, in order to participate fully in financial mainstream services, from free tax preparation to financial education, people with disabilities have reported that they need trustworthy information about tax services and filing; debt and credit counseling; savings and checking accounts; how receipt of a tax credit might interfere with their public benefits; and about the benefits of pensions and long-term care.

## Gateway to Asset Building through Community Based Partnerships and Free Tax Preparation

The Real Economic Impact (REI) Tour for Americans with disabilities is an economic model designed to end the connection between disability and poverty. The REI Tour is a public and private collaboration of over 14 national organizations and over 555 community-based partnerships in 84 cities for the 2009 tax filing season, committed to bringing low-income persons with disabilities into the financial mainstream.

The Tour is a response to the economic and financial service needs of those 22 million working-age Americans with disabilities. Despite legislation for civil rights, independent living, integrated education and the American with Disabilities Act, working Americans with disabilities have not been part of the new asset-building frontier for low-income Americans. Additionally, the growth of financial innovations such as matched savings plans and financial investment strategies has not addressed the disability market segment (as referenced above).

The REI Tour provides a long overdue roadmap out of poverty through public education about financial and tax education, participation in mainstream banking services, credit and debt counseling, and opportunities for homeownership.

Over the past three years, the National Disability Institute and the IRS Education Division, along with an array of other public and private organizations, have partnered to provide outreach and education to individuals with disabilities through the REI Tour. The 2006-2007 Tour reached

[1] May 4, 2007: Disabilities Research Report: Characteristics of Disabled Taxpayers Ages 18 to 59: Study of filing Patterns and Preferences for Receiving Tax Information & Services. Internal Revenue Service Wage & Investment Research. Prepared for Stakeholder Partnerships, Education & Communication. P. 14
[2] Ibid.
[3] Ibid.

over 36,000 Americans with disabilities in 54 cities across the United States. In each city, a local disability workgroup was created to address tax and financial needs of the community. To support this effort, NDI has created a framework for a website at www.reitour.org that is a resource center for the exchange of ideas and print materials that can be modified to fit the needs of a particular city.

## IMPORTANCE OF THE REAL ECONOMIC IMPACT TOUR

The Real Economic Impact Tour showcases the first-ever network of asset-building opportunities by leveraging existing partnerships among community-based free tax preparation and related asset-building organizations. Since 2005, the REI Tour, through a growing network of trusted partnerships provided free tax assistance to 151,751 taxpayers with disabilities with tax refunds of $136,374,700.[7] This money was reinvested into the economy of the local community. In 2008 over 90,000 individuals with disabilities were made aware of benefits in the tax code to which they were entitled and were assisted in filing their tax returns. The REI Tour also provides working individuals with disabilities on public benefits the opportunity to file for the first time. These individuals would not have filed and received these refundable credits without this assistance.

In 2006, the Ford Foundation funded a pilot program in four cities to better understand the tax and financial service needs of individuals with disabilities. Some of the key findings of this pilot program are as follows:[8]
- Thirty-five to fifty-percent of low-income individuals with disabilities reported little or no access to a computer with online services;
- More than 70 % of workers with disabilities were not aware of various tax and financial service information available online and more than 60% reported access challenges using online tax and financial services; and
- Taxpayers reported numerous barriers to doing their everyday banking – from teller windows that are too tall for someone in a wheelchair, to practices such as reporting a bank balance on a piece of paper for someone who is visually impaired, to lack of available voice-activated ATMs.

These findings suggest that there is a critical need for better integration of technology and education in the tax-filing process for people with disabilities. Although these reports are specific to the challenges taxpayers with disabilities experienced in accessing free tax help and financial services, anecdotal evidence provided by community organizations confirm that these findings carry a much broader implication for the mainstream financial service industry in expanding its outreach and education to clients with disabilities.

## SOME OF THE EMPLOYMENT AND TRAINING ADMINISTRATION'S EFFORTS TO PROMOTE ASSET DEVELOPMENT STRATEGIES IN THE NATIONAL WORKFORCE DEVELOPMENT SYSTEM

USDOL's Employment and Training Administration (ETA) has provided national support to promote asset development strategies. For example:

- ETA published Training and Employment Notice No. 5-07, issued July 10, 2007, "Real Economic Impact Tour TAX Facts+ Campaign Building Healthy Economic Futures for Americas with Disabilities." The document is available at: http://wdr.doleta.gov/directives/corr_doc.cfm?DOCN=2473.
- ETA sponsored two webinars on their website, http://www.workforce3one.org, to communicate the information about asset development and financial literacy for people with disabilities to the workforce investment system. These occurred on April 20, 2007 (title: "Real Economic Impact Tour: Building Healthy Economic Futures for Americas with Disabilities"; and February 21, 2008 (title: "One-Stop Career Centers: Assisting Asset-Building Programs for Low-Income Individuals with Disabilities.") National DPN Program Office staff, local DPNs (Jacksonville, FL, Detroit, Michigan, and Milwaukee, Wisconsin), staff from NDI, Inc., and IRS staff participated in these webinars. Over 300 people registered for each of these webinars and they are archived at the website.
- ETA staff has participated in several of the Real Economic Impact Tour's Leadership Academies (NYC, Baltimore, and San Antonio).
- ETA/DOL was one of the initial partners included in the "Real Economic Impact Tour: TAX Facts+ Campaign" to promote financial literacy, economic, self-sufficiency, and asset development for people with disabilities.
- The DPN Initiative's publication, "Resources of the Week," has included information on asset development for people with disabilities several times a year. This publication gets disseminated to over 15, 000 workforce investment stakeholders.
- DPNs are regularly queried about their participation in asset development activities and effective practices in the One-Stop Career Centers are compiled for availability to other One-Stops.

[7]Hartnett, J. (2008). Real Economic Impact Tour 2008 Report: Building a Better Economic Future for Americans with Disabilities: Annual Progress Report on the 2007-2008 REI Tour. [Release in October 2008].
[8]Ibid.

# NEW RESEARCH ON THE RELATIONSHIP OF WORKFORCE CENTERS TO LOCAL ASSET BUILDING COALTIIONS

In 2006-2007, the REI Tour built new relationships between local workforce centers or One-Stops and local asset-building coalitions. The REI Tour in Detroit, Jacksonville and Milwaukee all reported strong support from local or state governments, along with varied social service and faith-based organizations, to provide free tax preparation services. All three cities had major involvement of their Workforce Development system. The following three case studies highlight the possibilities for advancing an asset-building agenda to compliment employment services and supports.

## Detroit, Michigan
## Wayne County Asset Building Coalition

The Wayne County Asset Building Coalition (WCABC) is a program sponsored by the Michigan Statewide Earned Income Tax Coalition, with the Accounting Aid Society as the lead organization. WCABC provides tax assistance and promotes the economic self-sufficiency of low-income families, seniors and others in need through volunteerism and partnerships. Marshall Hunt, CPA, Director, Tax Assistance Program at the Accounting Aid Society introduced the program to the Detroit Workforce Development Center One-Stops five years ago and they have been involved ever since. The Workforce Centers are administered by the City of Detroit and are an agency of Michigan Works! the state's Department of Labor. Mr. Hunt reported that this partnership between the WCABC and the Detroit Workforce Development Center One-Stops fit well from the beginning, since the One-Stop deals with low income individuals and financial literacy on a daily basis. One-Stop personnel encouraged their customer base to use the free tax preparation and electronic filing services provided. Three One-Stops provided free tax assistance on eleven Saturdays with certified Workforce staff volunteering their time. The computer lab at the Workforce Center was used before the filing season to train volunteers. Accounting Aid Society provides the instructors.

One barrier reported is that the sites were not open during normal business hours for free tax preparation - only on Saturday from 10:00 a.m. to 2:00 p.m. on a first-come-first-served basis. However, this was turned into an opportunity by the volunteer staff providing free tax preparation. While individuals waited for tax preparation, One-Stop staff exposed them to employment opportunities. The volunteer One-Stop staff provided free brochures that focus on job seeking skills, resume writing, interviewing and spoke with individuals about what help they might need. Even though the doors closed at 2:00 PM, anyone who was already in the building was assisted. At the three centers there were approximately 20 Workforce Development Center volunteers and another 30 City of Detroit volunteers, who took turns staffing the Centers on Saturdays. During the 2007 filing season they prepared over 400 returns.

In addition, both the staff and consumer training centered on financial education and benefits. "Capitalizing on its unique relationship with its professional volunteers, business and financial institutions and its access to the economically disadvantaged individuals, the Accounting Aid Society began providing literacy resources and opportunities to open low-cost bank accounts to clients at its tax sites in 2002, forming the Financial Literacy Program."[9]  In September and October a mailing about the Earned Income Tax Credit was sent to all of the individuals who receive Temporary Assistance for Needy Families.  The One-Stops worked with banks and often have people available to help open accounts.  There is also a program that allows taxpayers to put their refund on a debit card.  Members of the Coalition come in on Saturdays and help to promote the services that they offer. *Even though the biggest concern of the taxpayers who come into the One-Stop Volunteer Income Tax Assistance (VITA) site is to have their tax return prepared and get the refund as soon as possible, by having other Coalition members at the One-Stop, they were able to utilize services of other community partners to access financial and/or social services.*

One of the Coalition partners, Wayne Metropolitan Community Action Agency (WMCAA), has for more than seven years operated the Center for Financial Asset Development, a One-Stop center for financial services, that runs the Michigan $AVE$ Individual Development Account Program, a statewide program that helps people with limited income to save money and build financial assets. At the Center they offer one point of entry for Individual Development Account (IDA), micro business development program, homeownership program, financial literacy, credit repair, and tax preparation services. Some of WMCAA clients are workers with disabilities who have successfully become homeowners.

The Disability Program Navigators (DPNs), (staff in over 40 states who help job seekers with disabilities navigate the local and state public systems of services) are also involved with customers in the One-Stop Career Center who are receiving services from Michigan Rehabilitative Services. The DPNs help them better understand the Department of Labor and Social Security Administration programs for individuals with disabilities and the interaction of the individual's current Federal disability benefits with potential employment.  The mission of Michigan Rehabilitation Services is to assist individuals with disabilities in achieving employment and self-sufficiency.  Michigan Rehabilitation Services (MRS) has one or more rehabilitation counselors at every Michigan Works! Service Center in the state.  The presence of MRS in the Workforce Centers helps to heighten the disability knowledge and sensitivity of partner agencies.

Public service announcements on radio, TV and cell phones, and posters and flyers are the primary marketing avenues for WCABC.  This flyer http://www.reitour.org/cities/docs/detroitMI/DetDisTaxPrepFlyer032407.pdf was widely distributed during the tax filing season in the Wayne County area and promoted the availability of banks to open accounts.

---

[9]Taken from Accounting Aid Society website: http://www.accountingaidsociety.org/pages/history.cfm

## FINDINGS

**1. The involvement of the Workforce Development System in free tax preparation began in 2002 when the Accounting Aid Society began a partnership with the System.**

The Accounting Aid Society, the lead partner in the Wayne County Asset Building Coalition, had been sponsoring VITA in the Detroit area since 1976. In 2002 they invited the Workforce Development System to sponsor VITA tax return preparation at their sites. The Workforce Development System in Detroit provides free tax preparation with additional resources through staff volunteer efforts for 11 weekends during tax season.

**2. The involvement of the Disability Program Navigator in the Wayne County Asset Building Coalition has made it possible to offer more outreach to the disability community.**

The partnership between the DPN and the Coalition, with the Accounting Aid Society (AAS) as its lead, has made available the Community Tax and Resource Center, a project within the AAS. This will link AAS tax services for low-income households with local community groups that provide asset-building tools and education. The goal is to help break the cycle of poverty and advance economic self-sufficiency.

## Jacksonville, Florida
## Real$ense Prosperity Campaign

The first organizational meeting of the Jacksonville coalition was held in December 2003 and the Real$ense Prosperity Campaign was ready for the 2004 tax filing season. Since that initial year the coalition has grown and increased services and outreach each succeeding year. The One-Stop Career Center joined the Campaign in time for the 2006 filing season. United Way of Northeast Florida is one of the major partners in the Real$ense Prosperity Campaign; a community coalition of 77 companies, agencies, government, educational, non-profit, and other organizations covering a six-county area. The focus, according to their website, which is located at: http://www.realsensejax.org/about.asp, is on "increasing the prosperity of our community by increasing the prosperity of each of our citizens."

The Temporary Aid to Needy Families (TANF) program promoted peer support and sponsored a workshop for people who are employed. The tie-in with economic self-sufficiency was mentioned as pivotal in bringing a number of the key community-based partners together such as the IRS, FDIC and local financial institutions. Local community-based partners such as the Real$ense Prosperity Campaign, along with United Way and the American Association for Retired Persons, played a critical role in helping the Workforce Development System build this movement.

The Real$ense Prosperity Campaign was the recipient of a small grant from Bank of America through the National Disability Institute. This grant was used to introduce the importance of serving customers with disabilities in existing free tax preparation outreach to the agencies already providing the service through VITA. This grant combined with the work of the local Disability Program Navigators in the Workforce Development System and provided momentum for outreach and inclusion of customers with disabilities in the self-sufficiency movement. The DPN has been a member of the Real$ense Prosperity Campaign Steering Committee since the Workforce Center joined the Campaign in 2006 and has been increasingly involved in every aspect of the initiative. The Real$ense Prosperity Campaign invited the local Independent Living Center to become involved as a free tax preparation site location. It was important that a site be disability sensitive and accessible. Sign language interpreters were included in this work as well.

The DPN conducts monthly orientations for job seekers with disabilities in each Workforce Center. The Disability Program Navigators and the Workforce Development System provide monthly disability awareness trainings at eight local One-Stops. Real$ense information is an integral part of the orientation at the One-Stop Career Center, with emphasis on EITC for adults (25+ without children and earning under 12k annually) and the FDIC Money Smart Program (financial education curriculum).

In spite of this, most participants report having no prior idea about the services and programs available. Information about free tax preparation and other asset-building opportunities was often not communicated effectively to potential customers with and without disabilities despite monthly trainings and dissemination of posters, brochures and fliers. It is vital in these sessions that front-line employees as well as state organization personnel (supported employment, Vocational Rehabilitation, etc.) working with individuals with disabilities are taught how to be proactive in getting the message to the public that assistance is available to them. They are trained to listen for cues such as, "I'm receiving SSI" that would indicate a person might have a disability and could benefit from the services offered through the Real$ense Prosperity Campaign and the One-Stop.

Disability specialists from the Center for Independent Living (CIL) and the DPN became Certified "Money Smart" Trainers. The classes are held year-round and are open to all individuals regardless of disability status. Those classes at the CIL do target people with disabilities and are totally accessible, including the availability of ASL Interpreters when requested.

Information on the Individual Development Account program was explained, including that the funds being saved and matched will not impact SSI eligibility and can be used concurrently with the Plan for Achieving Self-Sufficiency. The DPN has given presentations to the First Coast Rehabilitation Council and the Job Opportunity Consortium on the Campaign. Information was shared at the University of North Florida Disability Awareness Fair and at Tools for Success (a Duval County Schools conference for parents and professionals.)

Eight Workforce Centers hosted free tax preparation sites. Workforce staff members were trained and certified by the Internal Revenue Service and volunteer to do tax preparation on their own time in the evenings and on Saturdays. There was also a huge volunteer pool to staff the sites during regular working hours. The Workforce Development System provided 45 volunteers at eight sites for the free tax campaign in 2007. The Workforce Centers prepared 2,148 tax returns in 2007, a 43% increase over 2006. The 730 clients who claimed EITC received $1,118,957 in benefits. A local news channel hosted two information telethons, one in January and one in February, when a cadre of volunteers was present to answer questions about services of the Real$ense Prosperity Campaign and the Workforce Center. A DPN who took calls about the free tax preparation services reported she received so many inquiries that the Real$ense Prosperity Campaign extended the outreach.

One example of the success achieved by an individual with a disability is a young man who was facing multiple barriers to employment due to a physical disability. The DPN guided him through the maze of paperwork and he began to receive necessary training. After improving his social skills, the young man received woodshop training and now has a full-time job bundling and stacking wood. His commitment to surmounting life's obstacles and his determination to succeed has created a doorway to independence rather than giving up and sitting home in front of a TV set. Now that he is working he is motivated to learn more about managing his money and how to take advantage of the tax credits and matched savings programs available.

## FINDINGS

1. **The involvement of the Workforce Development System in free tax preparation was a response in part to the welfare transition self-sufficiency movement in the late 1990s.**

   The evolution of the Workforce centers into becoming integral partners in the local Volunteer Income Tax Assistance program is closely tied to the welfare transition self-sufficiency movement in the late 1990's. The welfare transition movement expanded employment services to include knowledge about financial literacy, free tax preparation assistance and other asset-building opportunities such as participation in a matched savings plan, homeownership counseling and many other programs.

2. **The addition of a disability focus to the self-sufficiency model evolving from the Workforce Development System was introduced by the lead community-based partner doing free tax preparation and through the addition of the Disability Program Navigator.**

   The Real$ense Prosperity Campaign was the recipient of a small grant through the Real Economic Impact Tour to introduce the importance of serving customers with disabilities in existing free tax preparation and outreach. This grant combined with the work of the local Disability Program Navigators in the Workforce Development System and provided real momentum for outreach and inclusion of customers with disabilities in the self-sufficiency movement.

**3. Most individuals contacting the Workforce Center reported that they did not know about free tax preparation and other financial education services available to them.**

This finding suggests that another mode of outreach – such as one-on-one education and the train-the-trainer workshops -- may be necessary to familiarize workers representing clients with disabilities, in addition to the dissemination of posters, and other print and media outreach efforts. Integrated resource teams where relationships are working are needed to support more people utilizing their local One-Stop.

Information sheet used by Jacksonville is available at this web address: http://www.realsensejax.org/materials/RSP_EITC%20Fact%20Sheet.pdf.

## Milwaukee, Wisconsin
## Milwaukee Asset Building Coalition

The Milwaukee Asset Building Coalition (MABC) is a program sponsored by the Social Development Commission, a Community Action Agency that receives community block grant funds. The MABC was established in 2001 for the purpose of leveraging community resources and community collaboration to assist residents in becoming asset owners. It emphasizes coordination of existing services, leveraging of community resources and enhanced community collaboration. There are 69 member organizations in the Coalition. Among the organizations engaged are the Mayor's Office, AARP, banks, social service agencies, and the job centers.

The state of Wisconsin mandated that the Workforce System collaborate with financial service partners, and the VITA program is one of those partnerships formed. The state set out certain guidelines for the Workforce System that have evolved over time. The Mayor's Office in Milwaukee has been designated as the lead agency for the Workforce initiative in the region while the Private Industry Council administers the Department of Labor (DOL) funds. The Local Workforce Investment Board has included education about Earned Income Tax Credit in their expectations for the Workforce Centers. There was a VITA site in one job center, and the DPN was instrumental in getting a VITA site in additional One-Stop Centers.

At this point one out of the five One-Stop Centers in Milwaukee has signed an MOU with the Workforce Board and the State. There are permanent Volunteer Income Tax Assistance Sites (VITA) in three of the One-Stop Centers in Milwaukee and a mobile site that serves the other two, but work is progressing on getting permanent VITA sites in all five. The mobile unit brings tax preparers and computers and sets up two or three days a week. Volunteers include employees at the Workforce Centers. They train either on site or at Social Development Commission sites.

The job centers have financial literacy training, which is also mandated by the state. Individual Development Account training is a part of the financial literacy training. The Private Industry Council sponsored a Financial Fair and cook-out in August 2007 with Mayor Tom Barrett as the kick-off speaker. Visitors included elected officials and representatives from FDIC Money Smart Program in Chicago. Over 400 people came to the Fair, receiving information on credit repair, tax preparation, checking, saving, predatory lending, identity theft, home buying counseling, grants for buying homes, car loans and financial literacy classes that are being held through the vendors at the One-Stops. The flier for the Fair is available at this web address: http://www.cr-sdc.org/SpecialEvents/Event%20Flyers/PIC%20Financial%20Fair.pdf.

To date the DPN is still receiving calls regarding the information that was given at the Fair, along with other agencies asking if one can be done for them! The emerging city collaboration with disability organizations, motivated by the work of the DPNs and the REI Tour, includes free tax filing, home buying counseling, financial education, and identification of contractors that will build accessible housing. Northcott Neighborhood House is a project that is on the drawing board and when completed will provide affordable housing for low-income working people, including individuals with disabilities. The plans for an accessible house were available at the Financial Fair in August for people to look at and ask questions. Goodwill Industries is the consultant to ensure that all residences are within the ADA guidelines. Disability outreach is done through the One Stops in order to ensure that individuals with disabilities are properly served there. The DPN is a certified Money Smart trainer. Her emphasis is on getting people in the door, whether they are working or not, to let them know what is available to them. For those that are currently working, help is offered to get them a better position. Every effort is made to make this truly one-stop shopping. By working closely with the organizations in the Milwaukee Asset Building Coalition the DPN has access to information about other programs that might benefit a person with a disability. Examples of such programs are food stamps and energy assistance.

The banks in the Coalition handle most of the marketing; they use radio, TV, and community advertising, etc. There are printed flyers advising of the availability of financial education and free tax preparation that are posted around town and available to all clients of the job centers. One point of emphasis is the Get Checking Program, meant to encourage people to better manage their own money and not depend on check cashing outlets. It is one of the primary methods used in credit repair.

The DPN is meeting with both the Independent Living Center and the Easter Seal Society for the purpose of establishing permanent VITA sites at these agencies. They are pushing for "independence first" as the guiding principle of agencies and community partners.

Milwaukee from the state to the local level has been committed to bringing its citizens full opportunities for employment and access to asset-building programs through its collaboration with free tax preparation and the asset-building coalition.

## FINDINGS

1. **The involvement of the Workforce Development System in free tax preparation was a response in part to the mandate issued by the state of Wisconsin and the involvement of the Disability Program Navigator in the overall Milwaukee Asset Building Coalition.**

   The partnership between the DPN and the Coalition has simplified the referrals to member agencies of individuals with disabilities who may be eligible for services not provided by the One-Stop.

2. **Home ownership for low income families, particularly those with disabilities, is a major goal of the MABC with the One-Stop Job Centers playing a significant role.**

   The focus on housing for individuals with disabilities has brought together partnerships in the city to facilitate the process from employment, to tax filing, to saving, then home buying and money management counseling.

## CONCLUSION

Americans with disabilities, practitioners working within the disability field, and tax and financial service providers want information and cross-training about asset development that is accessible, affordable, trustworthy, culturally competent, easy-to-understand, and that makes good business sense. Whether talking about complex work incentives, federal matched savings plans, disability-related tax provisions and credits, or financial services and products, the field needs trusted information that can be shared across both public and private community-based organizations. Recent reports to Congress[10] [11] from the IRS reaffirmed the need for more information and effective knowledge transfer strategies. The One-Stops are a key first footprint to offer reliable, free tax services and supports that are streamlined, accessible and accommodate taxpayers with disabilities.

This introductory research helps make the important connection between advancing employment goals and goals that focus on a better economic future. It demonstrates that there is a single most important factor in expanding outreach to taxpayers with disabilities so they can access free tax services and other asset-building programs. It is the development of on-the-ground relationships with community-based organizations that are not only focused on providing disability-related services. This research found that the local Workforce Centers are partnering with local community-based organizations providing free tax preparation. In some cities, as demonstrated in Jacksonville, Florida; Detroit, Michigan; and Milwaukee, Wisconsin; not only are the Workforce Centers providing the space for the tax preparation program, they are also providing a large volunteer pool of workers from the Centers. As this preliminary research demonstrates, when the Workforce Centers are associated with a Disability Program Navigator the combined efforts increase the capacity of the volunteer sites to service taxpayers with disabilities. In Jacksonville in the first year of partnering with the Workforce Center, volunteers prepared 9,937 returns, an 81% increase over the 2006 tax season. 2,198 returns qualified for EITC, an increase of 70% over 2006. Returns produced a total of $10,968,987, a 57% increase over 2006 returns. The involvement of Disability Program Navigators (DPN) in the local Disability Workgroups providing free tax preparation and financial education has been a win/win situation. The DPNs have ready access to many agencies providing outreach opportunities, and the agencies have access to an individual with knowledge of numerous resources for job seekers with disabilities.

The research found that many individuals with disabilities are filing taxes for the first time and are often unaware of the advantage of filing a tax return even when they are not required to file. This suggests that information about free tax preparation and the availability of Earned Income Tax Credit needs to be more widely disseminated to front-line employees in local and state public and private not-for-profit organizations working with individuals with disabilities, in order for them to be proactive.

When an analysis of promising practices was further reviewed across the three selected cities, three critical findings were identified:

1. The Workforce Development Center can serve as a hub for volunteer tax preparation assistance and for financial education programs.
2. Staff at the One-Stops can be trained to serve as volunteer tax preparers and to help connect job seekers with disabilities with other asset-building options.
3. The Workforce Development system is an important collaborator with other community-based groups and entities (for-profit and not-for-profit) that can connect employment objectives with longer-term economic self-sufficiency goals.
4. DPNs are vital conduits for making One-Stop staff aware of financial education and asset development opportunities for people with disabilities, and for creating the linkages that expand local asset development partnerships.

The implications in terms of future policy and program development are quite significant. Recommendations for future action include consideration of the following strategies:

1. Development of training and technical assistance to all One-Stops and state and local Workforce Investment Boards about the link between employment and asset- building tools and strategies, with an expanded role for the centers and DPNs as a hub for information, tax preparation assistance and financial education;
2. Creation of pilot sites to bring together disability specific agencies and generic groups, committed to implementing a comprehensive plan to advance economic self-sufficiency for working adults with disabilities that documents individual and system change and impact;
3. Identification of opportunities for policy development that stimulate a return to work, asset-building options, and more reasonable asset limits to continue access to major public benefits;
4. Assisting states in convening a work group at a state level to bring public and private stakeholders together to identify opportunities for collaboration with the workforce development system that would expand activities in the One-Stop. These activities could include but not be limited to benefit planning, financial education, access to EITC, use of IDAs, and braiding of funds in individual budgets.

---

[10](2007). Taxpayer Advocate Service, 2007 Annual Report to Congress — Volume One. Most Serious Problem #12, Outreach and Education on Disability Issues for Small Business/Self-Employed Taxpayers Internal Revenue Service. pp. 183-196.

[11](2007). Characteristics of Disabled Taxpayers Ages 18 to 59: Study of Filing Patterns and Preferences for Receiving Tax Information & Services. Prepared by IRS Wage & Investment Research, for Stakeholder Partnerships, Education & Communication (SPEC) Disability Initiative of the Internal Revenue Service.

**Information for this white paper came from:**
- National Center on Workforce and Disability/Adult (NCWD/A)
- Johnette Hartnett of The National Disability Institute; email address: jhartnett@ndi-inc.org
- Judy Stengel, retired from Internal Revenue Service's SPEC Office
- Michael Morris, JD of the Law, Health Policy & Disability Center, University of Iowa College of Law; and Director, National Disability Institute, Washington, D.C; email address: mmorris@ ndi-inc.org
- Office of Disability Employment Policy at the U.S. Department of Labor

**For additional information on Financial Education and Asset Development, contact:**
ODEP
1-866-633-7365 or 1-877-889-5627 (TTY)
http://www.dol.gov/odep

**For additional information on the Disability Program Navigator (DPN) Initiative and a list of state DPN contacts, refer to:** Division of Adult Services, Office of Workforce Investment, Employment and Training Administration, US Department of Labor: http://www.doleta.gov/disability

**Recommended Citation:**
Johnette T. Hartnett, Ed.D., Michael Morris, J.D., and Judy Stengel (9/2008). Creating a Roadmap out of Poverty for Americans with Disabilities: A Report on the Relationship of the Employment and Training Administration's Workforce Development System and Local Asset-Building Coalitions, For The Office of Disability Employment Policy and the Employment and Training Administration. (Washington, DC, US Department of Labor.)

**NCWD/A PARTNERS**
Institute for Community Inclusion at UMass Boston
Center for the Study & Advancement of Disability Policy
Law, Health Policy & Disability Center,
University of Iowa College of Law
Marc Gold & Associates/Employment for All
National Association of Workforce Boards
National Conference of State Legislatures
TransCen, Inc.